Hands-On History: Middle Ages

by Susan Kapuscinski Gaylord

S C H O L A S T I C
PROFESSIONAL BOOKS

New York ◆ Toronto ◆ London ◆ Auckland ◆ Sydney
Mexico City ◆ New Delhi ◆ Hong Kong ◆ Buenos Aires

For **Kendra**, a treasure and a delight

Acknowledgments

I thank Pat Beckwith, for her support and for the pleasure of working together, and all the students for their enthusiasm and good spirits as they embroidered, wove, made castles, donned costumes, and ate with their fingers off trenchers of bread. Special thanks to the following students who participated in our 2001 Medieval Week: Richard Adams, Bayley Ambrose, Alexandra Curry, Sandra Daaboul, Kirk Dillon, Kyle Johnston, Breanna Kostandin, Thomas Nelson, Kelsey Robbins, Brian St. Laurent, Tara Sonier.

Thanks also to Brendan Gaylord, Jim Higgins, Mike Prendergast, and Joan Ross for technical assistance, and to Mela Ottaiano for her editorial expertise.

As always, I owe it all to my family whose love, support, and tolerance see me through.

Cover design by Josué Castilleja
Interior design and illustrations by Susan Kapuscinski Gaylord
Interior photographs by Peter Bartkiewicz

ISBN 0-439-29642-0

2 3 4 5 6 7 8 9 10   40   08 07 06 05 04 03

Contents

Introduction 4

Who They Were
Getting Started 5
Who They Were 6
Heraldry 7
Coat of Arms 8
Design Planner 11
Charge Patterns 13

Where They Lived
Getting Started 15
Where They Lived 16
Castle 17

What They Wore
Getting Started 21
What They Wore 22
Costume Ideas 23
Circlet or Crown 24
Jewelry 25
Helmet 27
Circlet and Crown Patterns 29

What They Ate
Getting Started 30
What They Ate 31
The Feast 31
Saltcellar 35
Marzipan Subtlety 37
Pottage 39

How They Worked
Getting Started 40
How They Worked 41
Weaving 42
Craftsman's Sign 45

How They Played
Getting Started 47
How They Played 48
Nine Men's Morris 49
Embroidered Purse or Pouch 51
Embroidery Patterns 55

How They Learned
Getting Started 56
How They Learned 57
Illuminated Letters 58
Nameplate 59
Girdle Book 60
Illuminated Letter Patterns 66
Border Patterns 68

How They Worshiped
Getting Started 69
How They Worshiped 70
Stained Glass Windows 71
Miniature Stained Glass Window . . . 72
Rose Window 73
Stained Glass Window Patterns 75

Resources and Readings 78

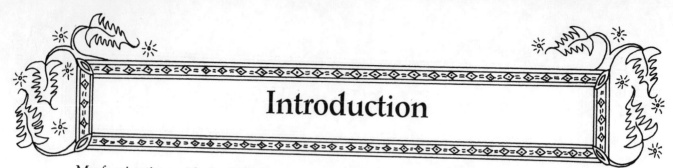

Introduction

My fascination with the Middle Ages started early and was very much connected to fairy tales and fantasy. In my young mind, I happily danced down castle steps in my flowing gown on my way to run through fields of flowers. My interest did not dim as I learned more about the reality. In the Middle Ages, which lasted from 500 to 1500 in Europe, the castle would have been dark and cold, life as a princess would have been a limited one, and the fields would have been tended by peasants with little or no freedom.

I passed my enthusiasm along to my children, again fed by fairy tales and fantasy, trips to museums and Renaissance festivals, and castles built with Legos. We have had medieval feasts for birthday parties and even danced around a Maypole on May Day.

When I had the chance to bring all of this into the classroom, I was thrilled. For the past ten years, I have been teaching bookmaking workshops on books around the world and across the curriculum. I finally had the chance to focus on the Middle Ages when I worked with sixth grade students at the Rupert A. Nock Middle School in Newburyport, Massachusetts. The experience was so successful I wanted to share the activities with other teachers.

This book is intended to be both instructional and fun. I am a firm believer in hands-on activities as a tool for learning, but I also understand the limitations of time, space, and materials in most classrooms. I have tried to make the projects as simple as possible, using easily accessible materials and basic techniques. I understand the importance of clear directions and simple steps, so I have provided as much detail as possible. While I have a fascination with things medieval, I am not a person who is particular about using authentic materials. I like to learn about the history and then work with contemporary materials in modern ways to make equivalent products.

In this book, you and your students will explore how daily life was lived in the Middle Ages. You'll learn who the people were, where they lived, what they ate, what they wore, as well as how they worked, played, learned, and worshiped. The book is divided into eight sections about each of these topics. Each section begins with a paragraph or two addressed to teachers where I mention aspects of the activities that were particularly appealing and aspects that some students might find challenging. The teacher page also includes a materials list for the related activities. Each section includes a brief historical introduction, which can be copied and shared with students, as well as step-by-step directions for completing the activities. The book ends with a section on Resources and Readings.

Getting Started

The project for this section focuses on heraldry, the method of identification for knights in battle. It introduces a theme found throughout the book: the importance of visual communication in a time when most of the population was illiterate. It is interesting that as we become a more global culture, symbols are again becoming important in communication.

Some students designed their coats of arms purely based on visual appeal, but most were interested in finding symbols that related to their names, interests, or characters. For students to find the meaning of their names, I used a book intended for new parents. Some students used photocopies of the *charge*, or symbol, patterns. Others used the patterns as a guide for their own drawings or created their own images.

Coat of Arms Materials

For each student, you will need:
◆ Design Planner (page 11)
◆ charge patterns (pages 12–14)
◆ pencil
◆ eraser
◆ colored pencils or markers (red, green, blue, purple, black, and yellow)
◆ 12″ x 18″ construction paper for shield or banner
   or 9″ x 12″ construction paper for tunic or tabard decoration
◆ pattern in the appropriate size
◆ construction paper (white, yellow, red, blue, green, purple, and black)
◆ scissors
◆ glue stick

✠ *Design Your Own Coat of Arms*, Rosemary A. Chorzempa. New York: Dover Publications, Inc., 1987.
You can find more information on heraldry in this Dover book.

Who They Were

In the Middle Ages, people thought of society as being divided into three groups, or *estates*: those who fought (noblemen and knights), those who worked (serfs and craftsmen), and those who prayed (clergy and monks).

The Middle Ages was a time of many small wars and continual fighting. If you owned land, you had to be ready and willing to defend it at all times. A system of protection called *feudalism* came to be. In return for protection and land, a nobleman gave his allegiance to the king and agreed to fight for him if needed. In the early Middle Ages, the nobleman fought with his own knights. As time went on, he was able to pay the king instead or hire others to fight in his place. Higher ranking noblemen would in turn give land to lower level nobles in return for their service.

Medieval society is often described as a pyramid. Those who fought and who had the most power were at the top. The wide base at the bottom of the pyramid were those who worked—the peasants who raised the food and did the manual work to make life possible. As the landowners owed allegiance to the king, peasants were similarly tied to their landlord.

Peasants could be either free or unfree. Unfree peasants were called *serfs* or *villeins* and they were required to work a certain number of days per week on the lord's land. They also had to pay the lord various fees and taxes. Free peasants, on the other hand, paid the lord rent for their land and owed him little labor and no fees or fines. However, obedience was still expected. While the serf belonged to the lord for his lifetime no matter where he went, if a free peasant moved off the land, he was no longer tied to the lord.

Heraldry

If you were a knight on horseback in the middle of a battle, you'd be wearing a suit of armor and a helmet. As you peered out of the eye slits of the helmet's visor, you'd see more knights who looked just like you. How could you tell whom to follow and whom to fight against? It was in answer to that question that knights began to paint designs on their shields.

In the beginning, each knight chose his own symbols and designs. He might choose an animal to represent strength if he were strong, refer to an accomplishment, or make a connection with his name. As time went on, the son would keep his father's design and add his own. The designs were also worn on the knight's surcoat, which he wore over his armor, and displayed on flags and banners carried in battle and hung in the castle.

With a whole slew of knights with different symbols or coats of arms, keeping track of who was whom was difficult. That became the job of the heralds. Heralds started out as messengers. In their travels they saw many different knights, all with different coats of arms, and they became experts at identifying them. Later, recording and keeping track of the different symbols became their only job. They would examine the arms of knights taking part in tournaments. Sometimes they even had the task of identifying those killed in battle.

In this activity, you will design a coat of arms for yourself. Like the knights, you'll want to make it tell something about who you are or what you like. It could also tell about your first or last name. It was during the Middle Ages that people first started to use last names. They were named for their parents (Johnson was John's son), their work (Smith was a blacksmith), or where they were from (Brook was the last name of someone who lived near a brook).

Coat of Arms

To make a coat of arms, start by working out a design on paper, then make a larger shield from construction paper or posterboard. Your coat of arms can also be used on banners and clothing.

The Shield

HEATER

The most common shape for a shield was called a *heater*. Women had a *lozenge*, which is shaped like a diamond, since they did not fight in battle. You can choose either shape.

The Field

The surface of the shield is called the field. It can contain different symbols or charges.

Tinctures

The colors in heraldry are called *tinctures*. There are three kinds of tinctures: metals, colors, and furs. Furs are drawn designs. For this project, we'll stick with colors and metals.

Metals

or (gold which is represented by yellow)
argent (silver which is represented by white)

Colors

gules (red)   *purpure* (purple)
azure (blue)   *sable* (black)
vert (green)

The early shields had only two tinctures, one metal, and one color. As time went on they became more complicated, but the rule was that a metal could not be placed on a metal or a color on a color. This was to make sure that the designs were easy to recognize.

Charges

On the field, there can be one or more charges, or symbols. There are *ordinaires* and *subordinaires*, which are geometric shapes, as well as images such as animals, flowers, fruits, sun, stars, castles, and buildings. These images had meaning. For example, a castle stood for safety, a lion for courage, a serpent for wisdom, and a bear for strength. You can create your own or use the charges provided. Ordinaires, subordinaires, and images can be combined on the same field.

Examples of Coats of Arms

The Design

Use the Design Planner to plan your design. Experiment with different ideas. These are just sketches; they don't have to be perfect.

You can use your design for a variety of things. It can be mounted on cardboard for a shield or hung from the walls as a decoration for a feast. A large one can be made as a banner; a small one can be pinned to your clothing.

Directions

1. Fold a sheet of construction paper in half vertically.

2. Cut a rounded point for a heater shield, a diamond for a lozenge, or a triangle out of the bottom for a banner. Use this as a pattern so that your final product does not have a crease in the center.

HEATER   LOZENGE   BANNER

3. Trace your pattern on construction paper or poster board and then cut it out.

4. Use your small plan as a guide and recreate your design. For large expanses of color, it is better to create your design by gluing one color paper on top of another in the collage method rather than by drawing with marker or crayon. This is much quicker and the colors will be solid and bright.

Design Planner

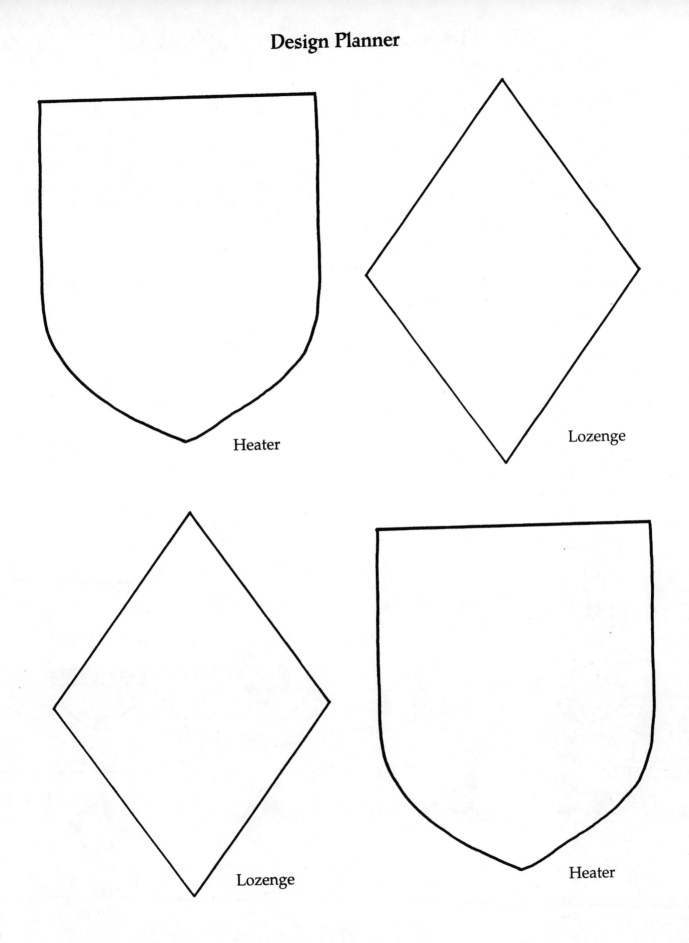

Heater

Lozenge

Lozenge

Heater

Charge Patterns (Ordinaires and Subordinaires)

Chief

Fess

Pale

Palets

Cross

Saltire

Chevron

Bordure

Pile

Passion Nails

Bend

Bend Sinister

Quarter

Pail

Inescutcheon

Bars

Roundels

Gyron

Lozenge

Mascle

Hands-On History: Middle Ages Scholastic Professional Books

Charge Patterns (Images)

Sun in splendor=glory and splendor; **Estoile or star**=glory; **Castle**=safety; **Harp**=calm person; **Tree**=new life from old; **Rose**=grace and beauty

Hands-On History: Middle Ages Scholastic Professional Books

Charge Patterns (Images)

Griffin=valor and bravery; **Serpent**=wisdom; **Unicorn**=extreme courage; **Bear**= strength; **Lion**=courage; **Eagle**=person of action and noble nature

Hands-On History: Middle Ages Scholastic Professional Books

Where They Lived

Getting Started

In this project, I let go of my usual compulsion for specific directions and worked with the students in an open-ended way. It was successful: the students loved building a castle and did a lot of creative problem solving in the process. We assembled a collection of boxes and cardboard and had paint, construction paper, and glue available. We had a core group of six students working together which seemed to be a good number. The construction took about three hours. I suggest dividing the class into groups to work on several castles, or enlarging the concept to include a cathedral or chapel, town, and peasants' cottages so that each group can work on something different.

Castle Materials

For each castle, you will need:

- ✦ large cardboard box with the flaps removed
- ✦ additional cardboard boxes
- ✦ long pieces of corrugated cardboard, about 6" high
- ✦ round tubes and boxes (oatmeal, cornmeal, and bread crumb boxes, paper towel and toilet paper tubes)
- ✦ paper milk cartons
- ✦ white glue (or glue gun with adult supervision)
- ✦ scissors
- ✦ utility knife (for adult use only)
- ✦ paper
- ✦ poster paint (white and black)
- ✦ brushes
- ✦ newspaper
- ✦ books with pictures of castles

Tips Before Proceeding

Gluing

Gluing the cardboard goes much quicker with a glue gun. White glue has to be held in place until it dries. A glue gun adheres almost instantly, but the hot glue can be dangerous, so I helped the students.

Cutting

Cutting large expanses of cardboard with scissors can be difficult for the students. I cut some pieces ahead with a utility knife and cut additional pieces when the students needed them.

✠ *Castles on the Web*
http://www.castlesontheweb.com
This commercial site has a well-organized collection of links including a Kids Page with games and student-created sites.

Where They Lived

If you lived in the Middle Ages, life would be a lot less comfortable than it is now. If you were a nobleman's son or daughter, you would live in a castle. If your parents were peasants, you would live in a small cottage or long house. Wherever you lived, you would have no running water, no central heat, and no electricity. You would bathe infrequently because water would have to be pumped from a well and then heated on the fire. Your home would be drafty and dark. You'd have mice and rats as frequent guests and you'd be annoyed by lice and bedbugs.

Because the life of a nobleman was very much about fighting and defending oneself, his home was a castle or fortress. Castles were often built on hills or cliffs to make them easier to defend. Early castles were made of wood, but wood was soon replaced by stone because it was stronger, more permanent, and would not burn. Towers were round so that attacking knights would have trouble climbing the walls. Windows on the lower floors were very narrow to protect against arrows. Castles were often surrounded by ditches or moats filled with water to make entry difficult if the bridge was drawn up.

Peasants lived in one-room cottages or long houses with several sections. In winter, they often shared their houses with the livestock. Cottages were most often built of *wattle* and *daub*. The wattle, woven strips of wood, was covered by the daub, a mixture of clay, straw, and dung. Most of the roofs were thatched with straw. The houses were not well built and usually lasted only thirty to forty years. The floor was dirt covered with straw or rushes. The few windows had shutters but no glass. There was a hearth in the center of the room and a hole in the ceiling. Because there was no chimney, the room was smoky. The one room was used for everything and there was little furniture as we know

Hands-On History: Middle Ages Scholastic Professional Books

it. Beds were thin mattresses stuffed with straw that were laid on the floor and the table was a board on stands called *trestles* that could be taken down easily.

The Castle

The castle was surrounded by a stone wall called a *curtain wall*. Sometimes there were two curtain walls, an outer and an inner. There were towers in the corners of the walls and also within longer walls. A *gatehouse* guarded the entrance. In front of the thick wooden doors was a heavy metal grate, called a *portcullis*, which could be lowered for protection. For further protection, the drawbridge, which crossed a moat, could be drawn up.

MOAT
CURTAIN WALL
TOWER   CHAPEL
KEEP
BAILEY or INNER WARD
KITCHEN
PORTCULLIS
WELL GATE- HOUSE
BARRACKS
STABLE
DRAWBRIDGE

The main building of the castle was the *keep,* which was where the noble family lived. The storage area was on the ground floor of the keep with the great hall above. The great hall was where the lord conducted the business of the estate and where meals and feasts took place. The kitchen was often in a separate building because of the risk of fire. The living quarters were on the upper floors. The room where the family relaxed was called the *solar*.

In the center of the castle was an open courtyard called a *bailey*, or *inner ward*. There was usually a chapel for worship, barracks for the soldiers, stables for the horses, and a well.

In this activity, you will make your castle from boxes. Look at pictures of castles in books to get ideas. The directions here can help you get started.

Making the Base

Use: Large cardboard box with the flaps removed

Method 1: The sides of the box will be the curtain wall of the castle. The floor of the box will have the keep placed on it, and the inside space will be the courtyard or bailey.

Method 2: For a castle built on a raised base, place the box upside down. Cardboard walls will be glued to the sides of the box.

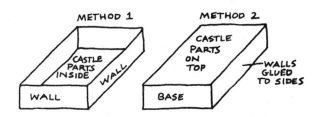

Making the Towers

Use: Round boxes and tubes (If you want the towers to have *crenelated*, or notched, tops, cut them first.)

Method 1: The towers fit over the corners of the base. Place the tube on top of the corner of the box, mark where the sides of the box hit the tube, and cut slits that are the height of the wall and a little wider than the width of the cardboard. Fit the tower over the corner with the walls inside the slits.

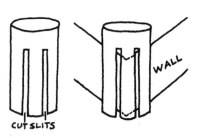

Method 2: Glue a tower to the top of the box in each of the four corners.

Tops for the Towers

Make a pointed cone top from a round piece of construction paper. Put glue along the top edge of the tower and set the cone on top.

Hands-On History: Middle Ages Scholastic Professional Books

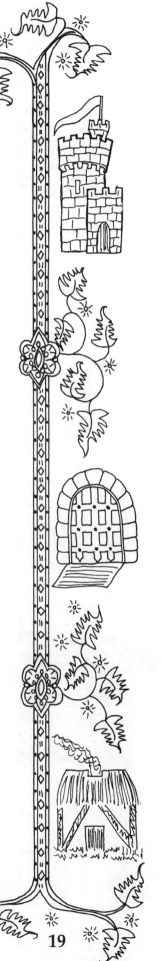

Making the Gatehouse

Use: Boxes or tubes for two more towers

Method 1: Cut two slits on the sides of each tube to fit it over the side of the box. Slip them over the wall about four to six inches apart. Make a gate or portcullis from construction paper and glue it on the wall, or cut an opening in the side of the box between the two towers for the entrance.

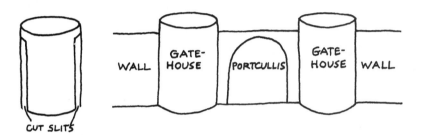

Method 2: Glue two more towers in the center of one side of the base. Space them about four to six inches apart.

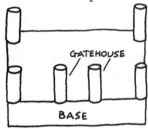

Making the Walls

Use: Existing walls or long pieces of cardboard about six inches high

Method 1: The walls should have a crenelated top. You can cut the cardboard wall that is there, but it will be easier to cut a narrow strip of cardboard, notch it, and glue it to the top of the walls.

Method 2: Cut notches along the top of the long pieces of cardboard. Glue these walls to the top of the sides of the box.

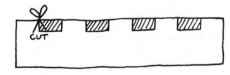

Making the Keep

Use: Rectangular box

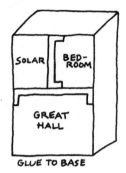

The box will be glued to the base of the castle. You can use it as a closed box so that you only have an exterior view, or cut away one side of the box so that you see inside the keep. If you want to add floors, cut pieces of cardboard, fold tabs down on two or three sides, and glue them to walls. The keep can be furnished. Hang banners from the walls of the Great Hall. Make small tapestries to decorate the walls. Make tables and benches out of cardboard.

Painting the Castle

You can paint directly on the cardboard or cover everything with paper (white glue works well) and then paint. If your boxes have writing on them or different surfaces, it is best to cover them with paper first.

To paint your castle gray, mix a few drops of black paint in a container of white paint. Slowly add more drops if you need to. To draw lines for the stones, wait until the paint dries and then use black paint and a thin brush or a marker.

Windows can be painted or glued on. If you cut windows from construction paper and glue them on, you can experiment with where to put them before you actually attach them.

Additional Elements

✦ chapel (another cardboard box)
✦ kitchen (another cardboard box)
✦ pennants (colored paper or cloth attached to toothpicks, bamboo skewers, or sticks)
✦ drawbridge (cardboard attached with small paper chains or string)
✦ moat (blue paper or cloth around the castle)
✦ people (decorated toilet paper tubes or clothespins set in clay bases, or use small dolls)
✦ well (toilet paper tube cut down)

What They Wore

Getting Started

Because I believe in keeping things simple, this section does not include any sewing. The projects are for the accessories: circlets or crowns and jeweled pendants and rings—worn by both men and women—as well as helmets.

We gathered a collection of long skirts, long dresses (old bridesmaid's dresses are great if you have access to them), scarves, and white and sheer curtain panels for the girls. For the boys, I bought inexpensive material, and folded and cut it to make *tabards*, or open sleeveless tunics. We focused on the dress of the nobles because there was more variety.

Circlet or Crown Materials

For each circlet, you will need:
+ circlet and crown patterns (page 29)
+ 3" x 28" strip of posterboard or oaktag (Gold and silver posterboard are available at some craft stores.)
+ pencil
+ scissors
+ stapler
+ markers
+ colored paper
+ plastic jewels and white glue (optional)

Pendant Materials

For each pendant, you will need:
+ cardboard circle, 3" in diameter
+ aluminum foil circle, 4" in diameter
+ aluminum foil circle, 2 $\frac{3}{4}$" in diameter
+ string
+ white glue
+ glitter or glitter glue
+ plastic jewels (optional)
+ awl or nail to punch hole in pendant
+ yarn, heavy thread, or crochet cotton

Ring Materials

For each ring, you will need:
+ 6" square of aluminum foil
+ white glue
+ glitter

Helmet Materials

For each helmet, you will need:
+ 16" x 28" piece of posterboard (black, white, gray, or silver) or oaktag
+ pencil
+ chalk
+ scissors
+ yardstick or long ruler
+ stapler
+ ballpoint pen
+ 4" x 18" pieces of construction paper

✠ *Medieval Costumes Paper Dolls*, Tom Tierney. New York: Dover Publications, Inc., 1996.
✠ *Knights and Armor Coloring Book*, A.G. Smith. New York, Dover Publications, Inc., 1996. These are good visual resources.

What They Wore

In the Middle Ages, all clothes were handmade. If you were a peasant, you would make them yourself. Starting with wool sheared from a sheep, you'd wash it, card it, spin it, weave it, and finally sew it. If you were rich, you would buy finer woven cloth and have a tailor make your garments.

The layered look was common in the Middle Ages. Underwear as we know it was not worn. Noblewomen wore a *chemise*, an undergarment like a nightgown with a long full skirt and long, tight sleeves as the first layer. This was the only piece of their clothing that was washed frequently. On top of that would go one or more long tunics. The first one had long sleeves and the outer tunic, or *surcoat*, was often sleeveless. Men wore an underlayer of linen drawers followed by one or more tunics. Their tunics were shorter than the women's. Because there were no buttons, all the garments were slipped over the head and often belted at the waist. The clothes were brightly colored and were usually made of wool. Sometimes imported silk was also used.

Men and women wore hose or stockings with slippers in the house and low boots outside. A mantle or cape lined with fur and fastened with a brooch or chain was worn outside. Women wore their hair long, often braided and coiled on top of their heads. They typically covered their heads with *wimples*, kerchiefs that covered the head and shoulders. Men and women also wore *circlets*, which were thin bands of metal worn around the head. As the Middle Ages progressed, the nobility paid more and more attention to their clothes. Just as they do today, styles came in and out of fashion.

Peasants' clothes were also of bright colors but they were much simpler. Peasants couldn't afford much and the clothes they worked in had to be comfortable. Men wore a short tunic belted at the waist and either short stockings like knee socks or long hose that fastened at the waist to a cloth belt. They wore a cloth cap or a hood on their heads. Women wore long loose gowns belted at the waist and wimples on their heads. Men and women wore leather boots with wooden soles. In winter, they wore sheepskin cloaks for warmth.

Costume Ideas

For Noblewomen
+ long dresses and skirts (silky fabrics, velvets, and brocades)
+ nightgowns for chemises to be covered with additional layers
+ long scarves
+ sheer curtain panels for veils to wear under a circlet
+ cords and sashes to wear as belts
+ wimples (Make from a cloth rectangle or scarf placed on the head and pinned to the hair.)

For Peasant Women
+ long dresses and skirts (cotton if possible)
+ cords and sashes for belts
+ wimples

For Noblemen
+ sweatpants, pants, or leggings
+ turtlenecks or plain shirts
+ tabards—sleeveless open tunics made from single pieces of cloth. (Make by folding a piece of solid color fabric in half. Cut a hole for the head in the middle of the fold. Attach a small version of the heraldic shield to the front with tape or pins.)

For Peasant Men
+ sweatpants or pants (dark colors are preferable)
+ long loose shirts (large men's button-down shirts with sleeves rolled up)
+ belts or cords

Circlet or Crown

Only kings and queens wore crowns, but many lords and ladies wore circlets of metal with or without jewels. Women often wore a veil that covered their hair under the circlet. Women also wove circlets of flowers in summer.

Your circlet will be made of posterboard, oaktag, or cover stock. You can decorate your circlet with markers, glitter pens, pieces of colored paper or foil, or plastic jewels.

Making the Circlet

1. Wrap the strip of posterboard around your head with a one-inch overlap and cut if necessary.

2. Place a pattern on the strip and trace along the top. You can use the one provided or make one of your own. Move the pattern and trace it across the length of the posterboard.

PATTERN

3. If you are drawing on the circlet or attaching pieces of colored paper, do so now.

4. Wrap the strip around your head again to double check the size. Then remove it and staple it.

5. If you are attaching plastic jewels, do so now. Hold the jewels in place until the glue sets.

Hands-On History: Middle Ages Scholastic Professional Books

Jewelry

Both men and women frequently wore jewelry—brooches or pins, rings, bracelets, and pendants. They were made of gold or silver with jewels. Because jewelry was expensive, it was a sign of importance. By the end of the fourteenth century most countries in Europe had passed *sumptuary laws*, which told people how much they could spend on jewelry and fancy clothes. These laws came about because the rulers didn't want others to look more important than they themselves did.

You can make a pendant and a ring from aluminum foil. The pendant has raised lines to look like metalwork to which glitter and jewels can be added.

Making the Pendant

1. Plan your design either on a separate piece of paper or by drawing it with pencil on the cardboard circle.

2. Use white glue to secure the string to the cardboard. Wait a few minutes until the glue sets. If you go on to the next step too soon, the string will move.

3. Put glue on the cardboard and the strings and place it face down on the center of the dull side of the larger foil circle.

CARD-BOARD
FOIL

4. Turn over the circle. Use your finger or the eraser end of a pencil to smooth the foil around the string.

5. Turn the circle face down, put glue around the edge of the circle and glue down the edges of the foil.

6. Glue the smaller foil circle to the back to completely cover the cardboard.

7. Poke a hole in the edge of the circle to hang the pendant. If your cardboard is thin, you can use a pushpin or the end of a ballpoint pen. If it is thick, use an awl or a nail and a hammer with a piece of wood underneath so you don't put a hole in the table.

8. Thread string, yarn, or thread through the hole and tie to make a pendant. Make sure it is large enough to go over your head.

9. Put glitter or glitter glue in the sections. If you use glitter, put the glue and glitter on one section at a time. Cover the previously done section with a piece of paper when you do the next. Add plastic jewels if you want.

Making the Ring

1. Roll the foil into a narrow tube. Squeeze and twist it to make it solid and strong.

2. Bend the foil around your ring finger so that the ends are even.

3. Remove the foil from your finger and twist the ends together and fold them down, shaping them to make a ball.

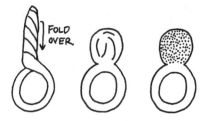

FOLD OVER

4. Put white glue on the ball and dip it in glitter.

Hands-On History: Middle Ages Scholastic Professional Books

Helmet

Knights wore helmets as protection in battle. They were made of metal and weighed as much as 25 pounds. Early helmets had eye holes to see out of and holes to allow air in for breathing. Later helmets had visors that could be raised to allow the knight to see and breathe more freely. Your helmet will be made from posterboard and will have eye slits and breathing holes.

Making the Helmet

1. Place the posterboard horizontally and draw a line across it three inches down from the top.

2. Draw lines about two inches apart from the top of the posterboard to the line. Cut along the vertical lines.

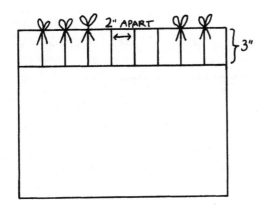

3. To mark where the eye slits go, have a partner hold the poster board in front of your face so that your face is in the center. Bend one of the center strips down and rest it on the top of your head. Indicate where your eyes are on the front of the poster-board (use two fingers for each eye

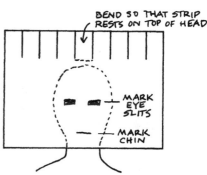

so that you can show the width) and your chin. Your partner should gently mark the eye and chin positions with chalk.

4. Remove the posterboard from in front of your face. Then draw the eye slits and cut them out. Poke holes with a ballpoint pen in the nose and mouth area for breathing.

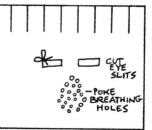

5. Have your partner or an adult wrap the helmet around your head. The helmet should be held together at the back while it is carefully lifted off your head and then stapled at the back.

6. Staple the strips at the top together by overlapping a couple of strips at a time. You'll have a small hole in the middle.

7. Cut two or three plumes out of the construction paper. Staple them to the top of the helmet so they cover the center hole and hang off to the side.

8. Trim up the two sides and around the back using the chin mark as a guide so the helmet will rest on your shoulders and extend a little lower in the front. Add another staple to the back if you need to. If the front piece is too long, trim it down.

Hands-On History: Middle Ages Scholastic Professional Books

Circlet and Crown Patterns

Getting Started

Our Middle Ages study concluded with a feast that the students loved. This section contains information about preparing a feast and recipes for two medieval dishes. I have tried to select recipes and foods that have a historical connection and that most students will consider edible.

This section contains directions for making a saltcellar for the feast, the standard peasant fare of pottage, and decorative marzipan subtleties. For the marzipan subtleties, I used both purchased marzipan, which is easier to work with, and "make-believe marzipan," which I adapted from a recipe in *Christmas Crafts* by Carolyn Meyer (New York: Harper & Row, 1974). Because it doesn't contain nuts, it is suitable for those with allergies. You can make the make-believe marzipan ahead as I did or make it with the students. Two rolls of purchased marzipan (available in baking section of most supermarkets) or one batch of make-believe marzipan makes about 24 one-inch subtleties.

Saltcellar Materials

For each saltcellar, you will need:
+ 2-liter plastic soda bottle
+ 4" circle of corrugated cardboard
+ scissors
+ masking tape
+ aluminum foil
+ decorative elements such as plastic jewels, sequins, metallic cord, or yarn, and white glue (optional)

Marzipan Subtlety Materials

For each student, you will need:
+ 1" ball of marzipan (from purchased roll or recipe on pages 37–38)
+ waxed paper
+ paper cups containing a few drops of food coloring mixed with a few drops of water
+ small paintbrushes
+ toothpicks or bamboo skewers

✠ *Godecookery.com*
http://www.godecookery.com
This large site has recipes, information about planning feasts, and period illustrations of food and serving.

Pottage Materials

For a pot of pottage, you will need:
+ Crock-Pot, saucepan with cover, or large bowl with cover or plastic wrap
+ wooden spoon
+ measuring cup
+ ingredients (page 39)

What They Ate

In the Middle Ages, food took a long time to prepare and, because there was no refrigeration, it spoiled easily. If you were a peasant, you'd eat a lot of the same food with very little choice. As the stored food from the previous summer ran out in late winter and early spring, you'd worry about getting enough to eat. If you were a noble, you'd have long meals with several courses every day, as well as elaborate feasts that would last for hours on holidays or when the king or other nobles came to visit.

Peasants raised and gathered their own food. Their main meal was either thick coarse brown bread or *pottage*, a porridge of barley, rye, or wheat to which beans and vegetables were sometimes added. Meat was rare in the peasant diet. The usual drink was ale.

The nobles had a much wider selection of food. Because the lord owned the forest, he could eat the meat of wild animals he hunted. He had all the rights to fish in the rivers and ponds on his manor lands. Peasants were severely punished for *poaching*, which is hunting or fishing on someone else's land. Eggs, milk, and cheese came from the farm animals. The nobles' orchards provided apples, pears, and cherries and their gardens were bigger than the peasants'. Raw fruit was thought to be unhealthy so it was always cooked. The food was more flavorful because the nobles could afford sugar and imported spices like pepper, cinnamon, and saffron. Wine and ale were served to drink.

The Feast

If you were invited to a feast in the Middle Ages, you'd pack your knife and go to the great hall of the castle. When you filed in with the other guests, you would be directed to a seat on a bench at a trestle table. The few chairs were reserved for the highest nobles. The host and the most

important guests were seated at a table that was on a raised platform, or *dais*. Trestle tables were placed perpendicular to the high center table to form a U shape. Everyone was seated by rank. The higher your rank, the closer to the high table you were.

The meal began when the Surveyor of Ceremonies, who wore a large gold key around his neck, welcomed everyone and presented the salt to the guests at the high table in an elaborate container called a saltcellar. The Pantler then served the bread. He cut the top or upper crust of the bread for the most honored guest. That is where the phrase *upper crust*, meaning upper class, comes from. Next the Ewerer came with a pitcher of warm water scented with herbs or flower petals, a basin, and a towel. Each person washed his hands as the Ewerer poured water over them and into the basin.

The highest nobles might eat their food on a plate, but everyone else had a *trencher*, which was a slice of bread. The bread could be eaten at the end of the meal, collected to be given to the poor, or fed to the dogs. Spoons were used to eat puddings and stews, and knives were used to lift pieces of meat from the platter and then to the mouth. Everything else was eaten with the fingers. There were no forks.

The feast took hours. A trumpet fanfare sounded as each course was served. Music was also played throughout the feast. There were three separate courses, each with as many as twelve different dishes. There were meats, fish, puddings, sweets, and pies. Some of the tastes would be strange to us. People in the Middle Ages liked combined flavors such as fish and venison (deer meat), beef with pears and almonds, and cucumbers with cinnamon and sugar. They liked their

Hands-On History: Middle Ages Scholastic Professional Books

food to look and taste interesting. They colored their food by adding parsley for green, saffron or egg yolk for gold, and violets for purple. They baked peacocks and then reassembled them with feathers and beaks to look like living birds. Between courses, entertainment was provided by minstrels, jesters, acrobats, and jugglers.

Planning a Feast

Seating
+ long tables arranged in a U shape
+ sheets or cloths to cover the tables
+ chairs for the high table, benches for the rest

Food
+ chicken wings, to experience eating with your hands
+ cheese
+ slices of apples or pears tossed with cinnamon and sugar, or served plain with a little lemon juice to keep them from turning brown
+ cucumber slices tossed with cinnamon and sugar
+ bowls of nuts (allergies permitting)
+ salad of greens with oil and vinegar dressing, and herbs if available
+ store-bought meat and vegetable turnovers and pies
+ cider
+ subtleties of marzipan

Serving
+ pitcher with warm water (can be scented with flowers or herbs)
+ large bowl for a basin to catch the water
+ towel for drying the hands
+ saltcellar
+ platters and serving plates
+ pita bread sliced in half to form two flat circles for the trenchers
+ paper cups with the sides wrapped in foil or goblet-shaped glasses
+ spoons and knives

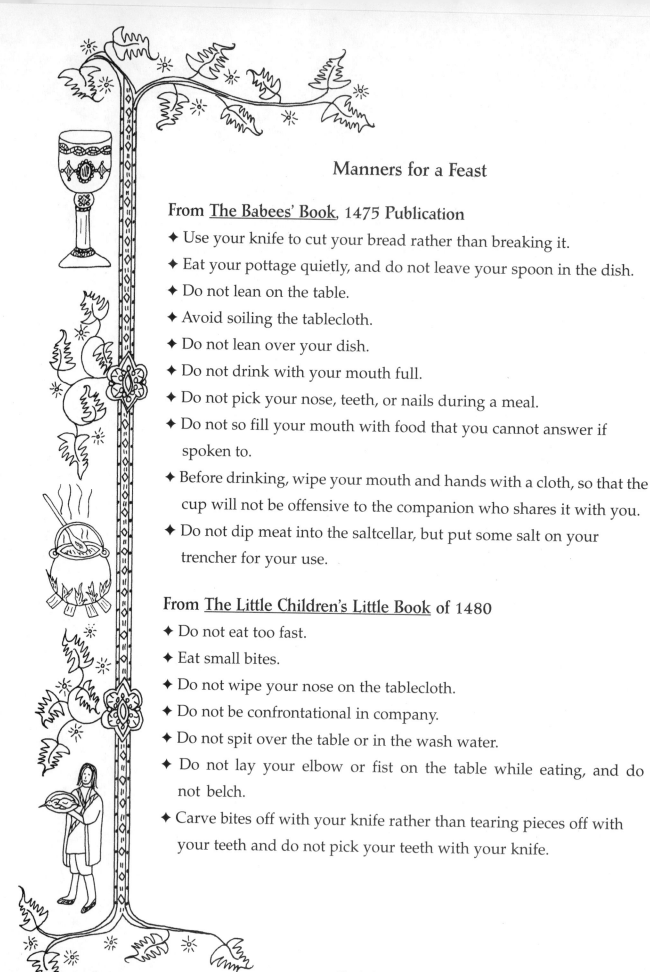

Manners for a Feast

From <u>The Babees' Book</u>, 1475 Publication

✦ Use your knife to cut your bread rather than breaking it.

✦ Eat your pottage quietly, and do not leave your spoon in the dish.

✦ Do not lean on the table.

✦ Avoid soiling the tablecloth.

✦ Do not lean over your dish.

✦ Do not drink with your mouth full.

✦ Do not pick your nose, teeth, or nails during a meal.

✦ Do not so fill your mouth with food that you cannot answer if spoken to.

✦ Before drinking, wipe your mouth and hands with a cloth, so that the cup will not be offensive to the companion who shares it with you.

✦ Do not dip meat into the saltcellar, but put some salt on your trencher for your use.

From <u>The Little Children's Little Book</u> of 1480

✦ Do not eat too fast.

✦ Eat small bites.

✦ Do not wipe your nose on the tablecloth.

✦ Do not be confrontational in company.

✦ Do not spit over the table or in the wash water.

✦ Do not lay your elbow or fist on the table while eating, and do not belch.

✦ Carve bites off with your knife rather than tearing pieces off with your teeth and do not pick your teeth with your knife.

Hands-On History: Middle Ages Scholastic Professional Books

Saltcellar

Salt was a valuable commodity in the Middle Ages. Because there was no refrigeration, food could spoil easily. Salt was used to preserve meat and fish. It also helped to disguise the taste if the food started to go bad.

In the Middle Ages there were no salt shakers. Salt was placed in a container called a saltcellar and served with a spoon. Saltcellars were often elaborate containers of gold or silver. Some were made in the shape of animals and birds, and some had covers. The saltcellar was placed on the high table in front of the guest of honor. People who were "above the salt" were of higher social standing than those who were "below the salt."

Your saltcellar will be made from a plastic soda bottle, cardboard, and aluminum foil. It will be held together with tape so it should be handled gently. You can make handles (for decoration, not for lifting) or shape it like a bird. Be careful when you work with the foil as it can tear easily.

Making the Saltcellar

1. Cut off the top of a two-liter soda bottle about three inches down from the neck. Ask an adult for help if you have difficulty.

2. Tape the neck of the bottle to the center of the cardboard circle with masking tape.

3. With the shiny side up, lay a piece of aluminum foil about 11 inches long over the center of the open end of the bottle. Gently push the foil into the bottle opening and make a curved bowl shape. Shape the rest of the foil around the sides of the bottle. Push it against the bottle to make it flat.

4. Make handles or a head or a tail for a bird from separate pieces of foil, shiny side out. Make the bottom of the pieces long enough so they can be taped to the sides of the bottle.

BIRD HEAD

BIRD TAIL

HANDLES

5. Tape the shaped foil to the sides of the bottle.

TAPE   TAPE

6. Place the cellar on a piece of foil about 12 inches long, shiny side down. Push the foil around the bottle to cover the base.

7. Wrap a piece of foil about 20 inches long around the cellar. It should overlap the top lip except where the handles are and go around the bottom of the pedestal. Push it against the bottle to shape it.

8. For the feast, pour salt into the bowl of the cellar and rest a small spoon in it.

Hands-On History: Middle Ages Scholastic Professional Books

Marzipan Subtlety

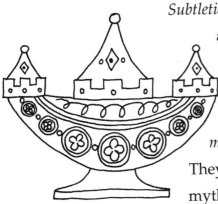

Subtleties were sculptures that were displayed at the end of each course of a feast. Some were just decorative constructions, but many were edible creations made from spun sugar, pastry, or *marzipan*, a paste made from almonds. They were shaped as castles, ships, animals, mythical creatures, people, and heraldic crests. In the Middle Ages, the subtleties would have been large pieces that were paraded through the hall. Yours will be a miniature one made from marzipan. They are so sweet that a little goes a long way.

Making the Marzipan

Ingredients for about 24 one-inch sculptures:

- ✦ 1 small potato
- ✦ 2 cups confectioners' sugar
- ✦ $\frac{2}{3}$ cup crushed cookie crumbs, such as vanilla wafers
- ✦ 1 teaspoon vanilla
- ✦ saucepan and cover
- ✦ mixing bowl
- ✦ fork
- ✦ mixing spoon

1. Wash and peel the potato, put it in the pan, and cover it with water. Bring the water to a boil, reduce the heat, cover the pan, and cook it at a low boil for 20 to 30 minutes until tender. You can also cook the potato in a microwave.

2. Take the potato out of the water and set it aside until it cools.

3. Mash the potato in the mixing bowl with the fork.

4. Add the confectioners' sugar a little at a time and mix it with the potato. The amount of sugar you need depends on the potato. You want a mixture that looks like creamy frosting.

5. Add the cookie crumbs and the vanilla and stir until mixed. You should be able to form the dough into small balls.

Making the Subtlety

1. Use your fingers to shape the ball of marzipan. If the marzipan is stiff, knead it in your hands until it is easier to handle. You can make fruits, flowers, animals, a miniature castle, stars and suns, or heraldic signs. Place the completed pieces on wax paper.

2. You can add texture marks by scratching into the figures with a toothpick or bamboo skewer. For example, you can poke little holes for the seeds in strawberries, make scale marks on a dragon, or indicate stones on a castle.

3. Dip a brush in a mixture of food coloring and water and paint the sculpture.

4. To keep them from hardening, store the subtleties in an airtight container or resealable plastic bag.

Pottage

Grain was the main food of the peasants. Many peasants made their grain into pottage rather than having it ground into flour for bread because when the miller ground their grain, he charged a fee of grain for both himself and the lord. Pottage was a porridge or stew of grain, with vegetables and beans added if they were available. Barley was a common grain and was often sprouted before cooking. It was cooked throughout the day in a pot or cauldron on the fire at the center of the cottage.

You can make your pottage on a stove top, in a microwave oven, or in a Crock-Pot—a modern way of doing the medieval slow cooking over a fire. You can use barley, wheat, rye, or a combination of the three. Vegetables can be added. Common vegetables in the Middle Ages were onions, cabbage, leeks, and turnips.

Making Pottage

Ingredients for 20 small (about $\frac{1}{3}$ cup) servings:
+ 2 cups of barley or mixed grains
+ $4\frac{1}{2}$ cups water
+ chicken or vegetable bouillon cube (in the Middle Ages pottage probably would have been cooked in plain water but the bouillon cube will give it flavor)
+ chopped vegetables (celery, carrots, onions, scallions or leeks, cabbage)

1. Place all the ingredients in your cooking pot.

2. Cook for two hours in Crock-Pot, 25 minutes in a microwave oven stirring once, or 30 minutes on the stove stirring frequently.

How They Worked

Getting Started

This section includes two activities: weaving and making a craftsman's sign. Making the craftsman's sign was a simple project that was easy for everyone to do. They chose trades from shieldmaker to greengrocer to tailor.

The students also found the weaving easy to do. The weavings can be made larger or smaller by varying the size of the loom. The warp (vertical) threads can be placed closer together for a tighter weave but the weaving is easiest with the warp threads one-half inch apart as suggested. I gave the students lengths of yarn about 60 inches long to work with. If the pieces are too long, they tend to become tangled as the students weave. If they are too short, students have to add new yarn too often.

The surprise to me was how much the students enjoyed the weaving, especially the boys. As soon as they finished the first one, they asked to do a second. Many brought their works in progress home and completed two or three weavings over the course of a week. I have a fond memory of a peaceful hour in which I read aloud while the students wove.

Weaving Materials

For each weaving, you will need:
+ piece of 8" x 10" corrugated cardboard for the loom
+ pencil
+ ruler
+ scissors
+ yarn in 60" lengths (a variety of colors and textures if possible)

Craftsman's Sign Materials

For each sign, you will need:
+ piece of 9" x 16" posterboard or cardboard
+ scissors
+ construction paper
+ yarn or string
+ pencil
+ markers
+ hole punch

✠ *Camelot Village*
http://www.camelotintl.com/village/street.html
Clicking on the people in a medieval street scene leads you to informative descriptions of the life of a peasant, lord of the manor, merchant, and more.

How They Worked

If you grew up in the Middle Ages, you would probably be working now rather than going to school. If you were going to be a knight, you would start your training in riding and fighting as a page at seven, become a squire who served a particular knight at fourteen, and, if you did well, be dubbed a knight yourself at twenty-one. If you were going to be a tradesman or craftsman, you would start as an apprentice between age seven and twelve. If you were a peasant, you'd be doing housework if you were a girl, and be out in the fields if you were a boy.

Peasants spent much of their lives outdoors. Farming was their main occupation. They worked in their own fields and in the fields of their lords. Except in the middle of winter, the year was busy with plowing, seeding, weeding, and harvesting. Women and girls did all the household work. They tended the fire, carried the water from the well, spun wool, wove cloth, made clothes, raised vegetables in the small plot of land outside the cottage (called a croft), prepared the meals, and preserved food for winter.

Craftsmen and tradesmen lived in villages, towns, and cities. They belonged to *guilds,* which were organizations of people who worked at the same trade. The guilds set standards for workmanship, made rules about the training of apprentices, and set wages. An apprentice—usually a boy but sometimes a girl—served for four to twelve years depending on the craft. At the end of the training, he would create a piece that would show mastery of all the required skills. That work was called a "masterpiece."

Although the noblewomen didn't cook or clean, they were responsible for managing the household. They planned the meals and directed the servants, who did the work. The noblemen supervised their estates but left the daily tasks to others. The *bailiff,* who worked for

them, oversaw all the farming operations from sowing grain to shearing sheep, collected rents, and made sure the peasants did their work. The *reeve*, who was elected from among the tenants, also had a hand in all aspects of the management of the manor.

Weaving

All cloth was made by hand in the Middle Ages and weaving was an important skill. Peasant women added weaving to their household tasks and wove coarse wool and linen cloth for clothing. Craftsmen weavers wove and sold cloth that was finer. The weaving was done on a wooden loom.

Skilled weavers also made *tapestries*, large illustrated weavings that were hung on the walls as decoration. Tapestries were preferred to paintings because they helped to warm the cold stone walls of the castle, and they were portable. A rich nobleman with more than one castle could carry his tapestries from property to property. They were made from wool, silk, and gold and silver threads.

Your weaving will be a simple one with a cardboard loom and yarn. It will be what is called a plain, or *tabby*, weave with an over-under pattern. While it won't have pictures, you can use different colored yarn to make bands of color. You can also vary the weight and texture of the yarn.

Warp and Weft

It is helpful to know the two basic terms of *warp* and *weft*. Warp is the yarn that goes up and down. It goes on the loom first. Weft is the yarn that is woven in and out of the warp from side to side. In the illustration, the warp is dark and the weft is light.

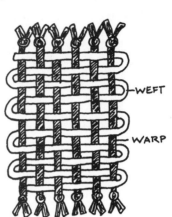

WEFT

WARP

Making the Cardboard Loom

1. Draw two lines across a piece of cardboard, the first line one-half inch from the top and the other one-half inch from the bottom.

2. Draw an even number of lines from top to bottom one-half inch apart.

3. Cut zigzags along the top and the bottom so the valley of each notch is at each vertical line.

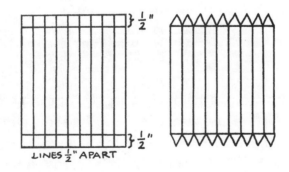

$\frac{1}{2}$"

$\frac{1}{2}$"

LINES $\frac{1}{2}$" APART

Warping the Loom

1. To warp, or thread, the loom, start at the back of the loom (the side without the lines). Leaving about a 10-inch tail, wrap the warp yarn around the notches in the cardboard. It should follow the lines in the front.

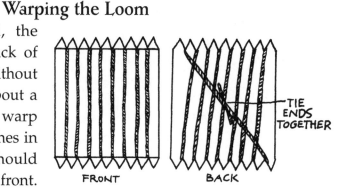

2. Tie the two ends together in the back. The yarn should be *taut,* or stretched tight.

Making the Weaving

1. Using the threaded loom, tie the weft yarn to the outside warp yarn at the top. You can start at the left or the right side. Leave about a one-inch tail so that you can weave the loose end in after.

2. Weave the weft yarn under and over the warp threads. When you finish the row, use your fingers to push the yarn up so that it makes a straight line at the top.

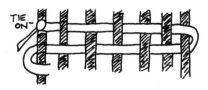

3. Wrap the yarn around the outer warp. If your last weave in the first row was under, the first weave in the second row will be over. If your last weave in the first row was over, the first weave in the second row will be under. Be careful not to pull the yarn too tight. You want to keep the side edges even. Use the pencil line as a guide.

4. Push up the row you have just woven with your fingers so that it touches the first row.

5. Continue back and forth, alternating the over and under pattern with each row. Remember to push the weft yarn up after each row and keep an eye on the side edges. It's very easy to have the edges curve in if you pull them in too tight.

6. To add more yarn or change colors, tie a new piece of yarn onto the old one. You can use one color for the whole piece or alternate bands of color, weight, and texture.

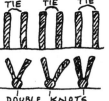

7. When the entire piece has been woven, cut the yarn in the back. Two by two, tie the ends of yarn together with double knots.

8. Trim the ends. Weave any loose ends into the weaving. Do it on the same side each time. That will be the back side of the weaving.

Craftsman's Sign

Because most people in the Middle Ages could not read, shops had signs with pictures rather than words. If you were a baker, you would 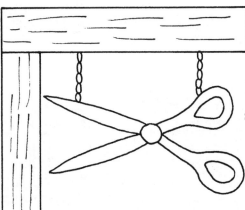 hang a sign outside your door with a loaf of bread carved from wood. A helmetmaker might have a helmet, a tailor a pair of scissors. In many towns, the same type of shops would be on the same street so that the street with the shoemakers would come to be called, for example, Shoe Lane. The houses were narrow and up to four stories tall. The upper stories stuck out over the ground floor. Most of the craftsmen had a shop on the first floor and lived above it. The streets were often narrow and dark because the upper stories blocked the light.

Some common trades in the Middle Ages were barber, shoemaker, helmetmaker, armorer, shieldmaker, swordmaker, blacksmith, goldsmith, silversmith, tanner, hatmaker, tailor, weaver, dyer, candlemaker, miller, grocer, oil merchant, pastry cook, baker, spice dealer, fishmonger, and saddlemaker.

Making the Sign

1. Using a piece of posterboard or cardboard, make a frame for the sign. It can be a rectangle with the center cut out or a piece with an overhanging bar. For the overhanging bar, fold the posterboard or cardboard about an inch back and attach the tab to the wall or bulletin board with push pins or tacks.

2. Create your symbol from construction paper, posterboard, or other papers. It will hang in the center of the frame, so make it an appropriate size. For a shieldmaker or armorer, you might want to cut the shape from posterboard and wrap it in foil.

3. Punch two holes in your shape and two holes in the top of the frame. Hang the symbol from the frame with yarn, thread, or string.

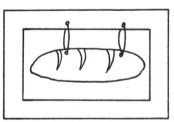

BAKER

SHIELDMAKER

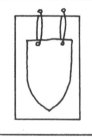

TACK TO WALL OR BULLETIN BOARD

HELMETMAKER

Hands-On History: Middle Ages Scholastic Professional Books

Getting Started

This section has two projects: a board game for two players and embroidery. There are directions for making the Nine Men's Morris board and how to play the game. If the players are evenly matched, the game can take a long time, so it might be helpful to set up a game area. The girls were the only takers for the embroidery in our group. I made a small sampler of the  different stitches to show the students. Some made the purse and others just enjoyed the embroidery itself and made several pieces.

Nine Men's Morris Materials

For each game, you will need:
✦ 12" square piece of construction paper
✦ pencil
✦ ruler to help make straight lines
✦ markers
✦ 2 sets of 9 counters (circles of different color paper or posterboard, two different coins, soda caps with different colored round stickers on them)
✦ 14" square piece of posterboard or mat board (optional)
✦ border patterns on page 68 (optional)

Embroidered Purse/Pouch Materials

For each purse/pouch, you will need:
✦ embroidery hoop
✦ embroidery needle
✦ embroidery floss (in different colors)
✦ 2 pieces of 5" x 7" cloth (an old sheet or lightweight cotton or muslin)
✦ copies of patterns (page 55)
✦ pencil
✦ thread
✦ scissors
✦ straight pins
✦ ribbon or yarn, 24" long
✦ safety pin

Tip Before Proceeding

To make a handmade embroidery hoop, use a large yogurt or other plastic container. Cut off the bottom of the container to make the bottom inner ring of the hoop. Cut out the center of the lid to make the larger outer ring.

✠ *Young Folk at Play*
http://www.ahs.uwaterloo.ca/~museum/Brueghel/
If you click on the numbers in Brueghel's painting *Young Folk at Play*, you can read descriptions of the games being played.

How They Played

In the Middle Ages, the nobility spent a lot of their time at play. With servants to do the household work and serfs to till the soil and raise the crops, they had a lot of leisure time. Tournaments or contests between knights were organized by great lords. They were both a form of entertainment and a way for the knights to practice the skills needed for battle. A tournament was a great social occasion, attended by lords and ladies who watched from the stands. Hunting, with dogs and with falcons, also provided entertainment as well as food for the castle table. Women often joined the men hunting, but spent much of their free time doing embroidery and needlework. Board games were common and included chess, checkers, Nine Men's Morris, and Fox and Geese. At feasts, entertainment was provided by jesters, acrobats, jugglers, and minstrels.

The peasants had long workdays and little time for daily leisure activities, but they took advantage of Sundays and holidays. They played running and tag games, in addition to board games like checkers, chess, and dice. Sports included an early form of soccer, as well as swimming, archery, and wrestling. In winter they skated on frozen ponds by strapping sharpened cow bones to their shoes. There were holidays in every season. Peasants were given time off from work on holidays and were treated to meat, cakes, and ale. The highlights of the year were the great fairs. The fairs brought displays of food, clothing, and household goods for sale by merchants and tradesmen, along with tournaments, jugglers and acrobats, traveling actors, puppeteers, minstrels, and musicians.

Hands-On History: Middle Ages Scholastic Professional Books

Nine Men's Morris

Nine Men's Morris was one of the board games played in the Middle Ages. Also called Merrills or Mill, it was played by two players with counters or pegs. The early boards were made of wood or stone. Such stone boards can be found in the walls of some cathedrals in Europe. It is thought that the stonemasons played the game while building the cathedral and then used the stone in the construction.

Making the Board

1. With a pencil and ruler, draw three concentric squares on a twelve-inch square of paper—the first square one inch in from the edges, the second two and one-half inches in, and the third four inches in.

2. Draw circles in the four corners of each square and in the middle of each side. The circles should be three-fourths to one inch in diameter.

3. Outline or color in the circles with a marker or cut paper circles and glue them on. They should all be the same color.

4. Trace over the lines between the circles with a marker.

5. For a sturdier board, mount it on a piece of posterboard or mat board You can decorate the edges with a border of your own design, use one of the designs provided, or leave the edges plain.

Playing the Game

Each player has nine counters. The object of the game is to get three of your counters in a row along a line called a mill. This allows you to take a counter from your opponent. You win when your opponent has only two counters left on the board or when you have cornered all the opposing counters so that they cannot be moved. A warning: it's not as easy as it sounds. You have to do some real thinking to play this game.

1. Take turns placing the counters on the board one at a time, trying to get a mill. A player who makes a line of three gets to remove one counter from his opponent.

2. When all the counters have been placed, take turns moving one counter along any line to the adjacent unoccupied circle, always trying to get a line of three so that an opposing counter can be removed.

3. The winner is the player who has taken away seven counters from her opponent, so that there are only two counters left on the board, or corners all the opposing counters so that they cannot be moved.

Hands-On History: Middle Ages Scholastic Professional Books

Embroidered Purse or Pouch

If you were the daughter of a lord and lady, you would be expected to learn how to embroider. As a lady, you would spend much of your leisure time with needle and thread. The embroidery was done with wool, silk, and metallic threads on linen cloth. The colors were made by dyeing the thread with different plants. The patterns were usually provided by professional designers. The ladies decorated garments for the clergy and wall hangings for the church, as well as clothes for themselves, bed hangings for the castle, and accessories such as purses and pouches.

Because clothes in the Middle Ages had no pockets, both men and women wore pouches and purses which hung from their belts. Men might carry important papers in their pouch; women their sewing tools. They did not carry money as often as we do today. There was no paper money and the main type of coin was a silver penny.

Your purse or pouch will have an embroidered design on the front and a drawstring with which to close the bag and hang it from a belt.

Making the Embroidery

1. Create the design for your embroidery. Draw your own on a piece of paper or use the patterns provided.

2. Tape one piece of the cloth to the paper with the design. The design should be in the center of the cloth and the bottom of the design should be about one and one-half inches above the bottom of the cloth. Trace the design on the cloth with pencil.

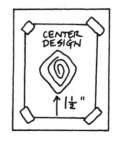

3. Insert the fabric in the hoop so the design is visible.

4. Embroidery floss is made up of six strands. You can use all six strands or separate them, using two or three at a time. Use pieces that are about 24 inches long. Thread the needle and overlap the thread about two inches. Tie a knot at the end.

5. Use any of the following stitches to create the design in embroidery. You can use different kinds of stitches and change colors. Always start from the underside of the hoop so the knot doesn't show. Be careful not to pull the thread too tight as you sew, or the cloth will pucker.

Running Stitch

The running stitch makes a broken line. The stitches on the top and bottom should be the same size. You can vary the look of the different lines by changing the size of the stitches.

Hands-On History: Middle Ages Scholastic Professional Books

Backstitch

The backstitch makes a solid line. It is similar to the running stitch except that you go back and fill in the spaces. There is a double layer of thread on the underside of the cloth.

Chain Stitch

This stitch is attractive but a little harder. To start, bring the needle to the right side of the cloth. Insert the needle in the cloth right next to where it came out. Loop the  thread under the needle as you make a stitch. As you pull the thread it will form a loop. Put the needle back in the cloth inside the loop and close to the last stitch. Make another stitch and loop the thread under the needle. At the end, anchor it by making a small stitch over the end of the last loop.

Satin Stitch

Satin stitches are straight stitches that are worked very closely together to fill in a solid shape. The threads are side by side, but do not overlap.

To Tie Off at the End

From the underside, slip the needle under the previous stitch and pull through leaving a loop. Slip the needle under the loop and pull until tight. Trim the end, leaving about three-fourths inch of thread.

Making the Purse or Pouch

1. Place the two pieces of cloth face to face with the embroidered design on the inside.

2. Pin the pieces together.

3. Starting one inch down from the top, sew around the sides of the purse with a running stitch about one-fourth inch in from the edge. End one inch before the top on the other side.

4. To make the tube for the drawstring, fold over the edge of the cloth about one-eighth inch. Fold it again to meet the place where the sides are stitched. Pin along the bottom of the tube and sew. Start with the knot on the front side which is the inside of the purse.

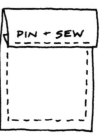

5. Turn the purse over and do the same on the other side.

6. Turn it inside out so the design is on the outside.

7. Tie the ribbon or yarn to a safety pin that is small enough to fit through the tube. Thread it through the front tube from right to left, and then through the back tube from left to right. Tie the two ends together.

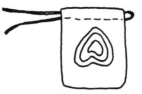

Hands-On History: Middle Ages Scholastic Professional Books

Embroidery Patterns

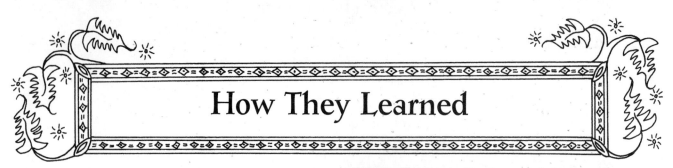

Getting Started

The students in our groups liked both of the activities in this section. The illuminated letter nameplates were a big hit. The students used the letter outlines provided and decorated them with colored pencils and markers.

The girdle book activity can be completed in two sessions of 40 to 45 minutes—one for sewing the book together and one for making the girdle cover. The sewing can be done with the whole class working together if you have enough tools, or in small groups if you don't. I have sewing kits in resealable bags containing a needle, clothespins, a pushpin, and a small piece of cardboard. I use tapestry needles for safety (they have a dull point) and ease of use (the large eye makes for easy threading). Our students used their books as journals but they can also be used for research and creative writing. The illuminated letters can be reduced on a copier and used in the book.

Illuminated Letters Materials

For each student, you will need:

+ letter patterns (pages 66–67)
+ border patterns (page 68)
+ construction paper, mat board, or posterboard
+ colored markers and pencils
+ scissors
+ glue stick

✠ *Leaves of Gold: Treasures from Philadelphia Collections Learning Center*
http://www.leavesofgold.org/learn/index.html
Written for students, this is a thorough site with a section on how manuscripts are made, a slide show of manuscript pages and descriptions, a glossary of terms, and instructions for teachers.

Girdle Book Materials

For each book, you will need:

+ 4 to 8 sheets $5\frac{1}{2}''$ x $8\frac{1}{2}''$ paper (Each sheet makes four pages.)
+ 1 piece of $5\frac{3}{4}''$ x $8\frac{3}{4}''$ oaktag or cover stock
+ 1 piece of 18″ crochet cotton, dental floss, or heavy thread
+ 1 brown grocery bag
+ 2 half-inch pieces of tan Velcro
+ scissors
+ 2 clothespins or paper clips
+ pushpin
+ small piece of cardboard
+ tapestry needle
+ white glue
+ pencil
+ brown crayon (optional)

How They Learned

The time we live in is often called the Information Age because it's easy to find information on the Internet, in an encyclopedia, or at the library. In the Middle Ages, the information you needed came from your elders. If you were a peasant, you needed to know how to work a plow and how to sow and harvest grain. If you wanted to be a craftsman, you'd learn your craft from a master. You wouldn't need books and you wouldn't need to know how to read.

Sons of noblemen learned how to read and write so that they could conduct the business of the estate and understand legal documents. They were tutored at home or sent to school. Because the eldest son inherited all of his father's property, other sons were left without any land. Some became knight errants who traveled around fighting in tournaments and for other noblemen. Some went to monasteries and trained to become priests. Others studied to become government officials or teachers. Daughters were taught by their mothers or by nuns. They needed to be able to read and do math so they could manage the large household in the castle.

In the early Middle Ages, books were very rare and found mostly in monastery libraries. Every book was made by hand. The monks who did the writing were called *scribes*, and the room they worked in was called a *scriptorium*. The pages were made from *vellum*, which is calfskin, or *parchment*, which is sheepskin or goatskin. The writing was done with a reed for large letters and a quill for smaller ones. All the books were written in Latin. The covers were made of thick boards and sometimes were covered with ornate metalwork and encrusted with jewels. Many of the books were so valuable that they were chained to their shelves.

Eventually books were found in places other than monasteries. Noblemen hired scribes and illuminators to make books for them and their wives. Medieval best sellers were Books of Hours, which had prayers to read throughout the day. When universities opened, books were produced for them. After Johannes Gutenberg began printing with movable type in 1450, books became more plentiful, although the majority of people still did not know how to read.

Illuminated Letters

When you read a book, you know when a new chapter starts because there is a heading and a number. You know when a new topic starts, because the words are indented to form a paragraph. In the Middle Ages, books did not have title pages, chapter headings, or indentations for what we would call paragraphs. Instead, the first letters of the book, the chapters, and the paragraphs were made larger and decorated with gold leaf and paint. Because they added color and brightness to the page, they were called illuminated letters.

The manuscript was written first by the scribe or scribes who left spaces for the illuminated initials. The *illuminator* sketched his drawing with a lead or metal point. The gold was applied next. Finally, the colors, which were made from pigments from plants and minerals combined with egg, were painted on with a brush.

Illuminated Letter Nameplate

Spell out your name with illuminated letters. Use the patterns provided for the letters or draw your own. Decorate the letters. Make them represent you by using your favorite colors and drawing pictures that tell about your favorite pastimes, sports, or pets. Mount the letters on construction paper, posterboard, or mat board. You can add borders by using the patterns provided or by drawing your own.

You can also use the letters as an initial letter in a page of poetry, as paragraph markings in a research report, or in a girdle book.

Girdle Book

If you were a monk in the Middle Ages, you'd want to be able to read your book of prayers anytime. But because you wouldn't want to have your hands full carrying around a book, you'd have a girdle book. A *girdle* was a belt or cord worn around the waist. A *girdle book* had a long cover with a knot or knob on the top that could be tucked under the girdle. The cover was usually made of doeskin or deerskin held together with leather straps and metal clasps. The monk could lift his book and read it as he walked or stood. Noblemen and women also had girdle books of prayers. Some girdle books had covers of velvet decorated with embroidery.

Your girdle book will use a brown grocery bag instead of leather and Velcro instead of metal clasps. If you remember how to cover your books at the beginning of the school year, this will be easy.

Making the Book

1. After tapping all your sheets of paper together to make an even stack, fold them in half, being careful to line up the corners.

2. Fold the cover piece in half.

3. Insert the paper into the cover. The cover is a little larger. There should be an even amount of cover showing on the top and bottom, and the folds of the paper should match up with the fold of the cover. With the clothespins, clip it at the top on the right side of the fold and at the bottom on the left.

Hands-On History: Middle Ages Scholastic Professional Books

4. Make three holes along the fold with the pushpin—one in the center, one about an inch from the top, and one about an inch from the bottom. Place the cardboard underneath so that the pin will go into it and not your desk.

5. Thread the needle. Tie the thread onto the needle so it won't slip out as you sew. Do not tie a knot at the end and leave the strand single.

6. Enter into the center hole from the inside of the book. Pull the thread through and place the end under the bottom clothespin.

7. The thread is on the outside now. Go up to and through the top hole.

8. You're back on the inside again. Go down to and through the bottom hole.

9. You're on the outside. Go through the center hole.

10. Arrange the thread so that the two ends go out to the sides and the long center stitch is on the top. Pull the ends gently but firmly to make sure the thread is taut. Tie the two ends of the thread in a double knot. A square knot (right over left, left over right) is preferable.

11. Trim the ends of the thread to about one inch long. If you cut the ends too short, the knot may unravel.

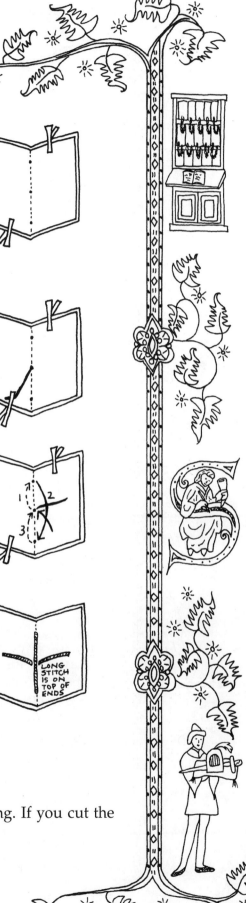

Making the Girdle Cover

1. Cut down the center side fold of both sides of a grocery bag and then cut off the bottom. You will be using the side without the writing for the cover.

2. To soften the paper and make it seem more like leather, take a fistful of paper in each hand and rub your hands together. It will take a while as you'll be doing a section at a time. Then smooth out the paper with the palm of your hand. If you wish to deepen the color, rub the side of a brown crayon across the paper.

3. Hold the paper in front of you so that it is taller than it is wide and fold it in half so that it is long and skinny. Run your hand along the crease to flatten it.

4. Open the paper.

5. Fold the bottom edge up to make a two-inch flap.

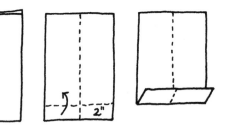

6. Lay the closed book on the bag so that the spine of the book (where the stitching is) is on the center crease and the bottom of the book is even with the bottom folded edge of the bag.

7. Open the front cover of the book. Fold the edge of the bag over the cover and crease it.

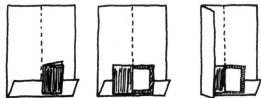

Hands-On History: Middle Ages Scholastic Professional Books

8. Lift the edge you just folded and insert the front cover between it and the bottom flap that you folded up before.

9. Flip the pages over to the left so that the back cover is free and do the same thing.

10. Place the book so that the fold is on the left and it opens on the right.

11. Put white glue on the top three to four inches of the bag cover. Fold over the right and left sides to form a narrow strip about two inches wide. Press to help it stick.

12. Put white glue on the narrow strip. Roll the strip down and squeeze and twist it in your fist to make a knob.

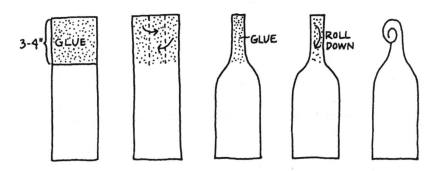

13. Remove the book from the cover. It might get stuck to the cover when you put the straps and clasps on next and you'll find it is much easier to write in the book when it is out of the cover.

Making the Straps and Clasps

1. Cut two 2" x 2" pieces from the leftover piece of the grocery bag.

2. Fold each piece into thirds. Open, apply glue, and refold. Squeeze to make sure the glue sticks. These will be the straps.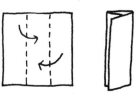

3. If you want, shape the ends of the straps. Draw on clasps on the outside of them.

4. On the side edge of the back cover, make two pencil marks on the side crease of the back cover, one at one and one-half inches from the bottom and one at four inches from the bottom.

5. At each mark, trim the side edge of the back cover to make a slit big enough for the strap to fit through.

6. Put glue on the top one-half inch of the straps and insert them into the slits with the glue toward the outside of the cover. Press to help the glue adhere.

7. Peel the protective covering off one side of a piece of Velcro and attach it to the underside of one of the straps. Peel the protective covering off the other side, close the clasp over the book, and press to make it stick. Do the same for the other strap.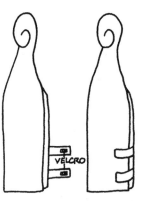

Using the Girdle Book

Do your writing with the book outside the cover—it will be much easier to work this way. When you are finished, insert the book into the girdle cover upside down so that you can read it while it is tucked under a belt.

You might use your girdle book as a journal about your study of the Middle Ages, or to write an imaginary diary of a boy or girl during that time. You could write your experiences as a page, a young girl at home in the castle, or a peasant child. You could write a diary of a character from the Middle Ages, such as King Arthur or one of the Knights of the Round Table, Guinevere, Robin Hood, Joan of Arc, or Eleanor of Aquitaine.

Books of Hours were often made as girdle books. They had prayers to read throughout the day and a calendar of the year with the saints' days. Many of them also had illustrations which showed daily life in each month of the year. You could make a book with a section for each month or season of the year and describe what the nobles and the peasants would have done, from planting and harvesting to hunting and feasting. If you use seven sheets of paper, you will have a title page and two pages for each month of the year.

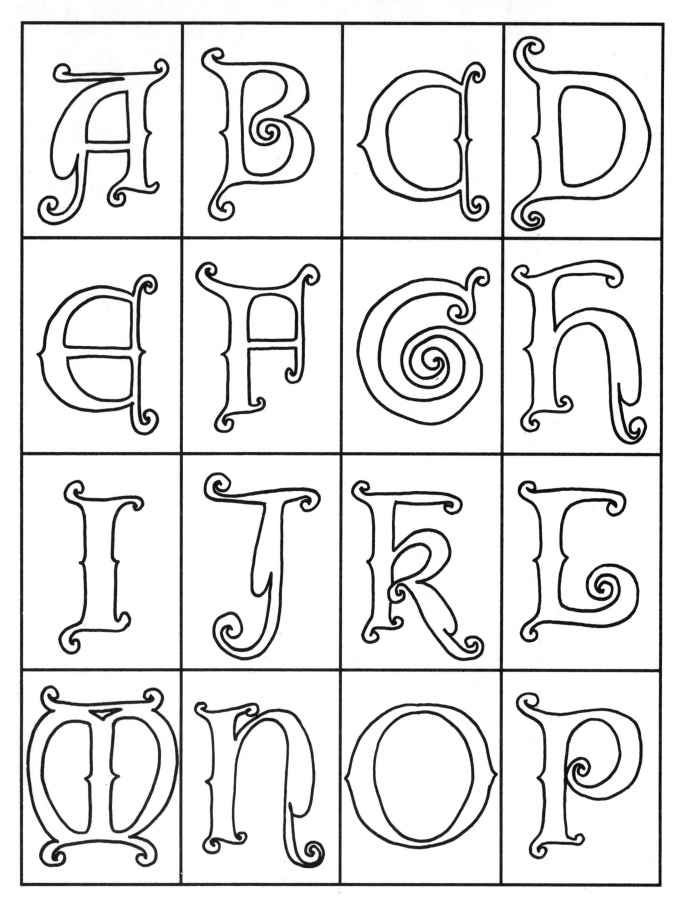

Hands-On History: Middle Ages Scholastic Professional Books

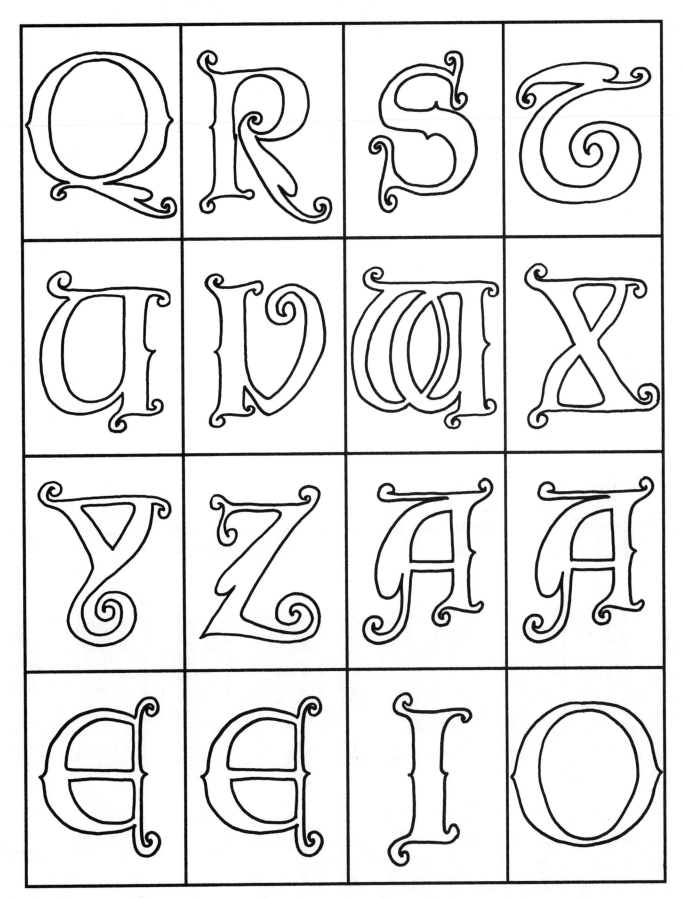

Border Patterns

Hands-On History: Middle Ages Scholastic Professional Books

How They Worshiped

Getting Started

In this section, the activities are a miniature stained glass window that each student can easily make alone, and a larger one made from posterboard and tissue paper. The miniature stained glass is made from transparency film and is colored with waterproof markers. The colors are bright and stay on the slick surface, but will fade after a prolonged time in the window. If you don't have easy access to waterproof markers, you can mix poster paint with a drop of dishwashing liquid and put the color on with a brush. The students spent about an hour on the small window and enjoyed both the process and the finished product.

The larger rose window works best with two students working together. It was difficult to poke holes in the posterboard to start cutting out the sections, so I did that. Some of the students had difficulty cutting as well, and we gave that task to those who were good with scissors.

Miniature Stained Glass Materials

For each window, you will need:
+ 1 piece of $4\frac{1}{4}$" x $5\frac{1}{2}$" transparency film
  (used with overhead projectors)
+ 2 pieces of 5" x 7" black posterboard
+ patterns for window frames (pages 75–76)
+ Stained Glass patterns (page 77)
+ pencil
+ scissors
+ transparent tape
+ waterproof markers in black and
  various colors
+ white glue
+ ribbon or yarn (optional)

Rose Window Materials

For a large rose window, you will need:
+ 2 sheets of black posterboard*
+ tissue paper in a variety of colors
+ pencil
+ scissors
+ white glue
+ ruler to help make straight lines (optional)
+ masking tape

*You can make a smaller window out of one sheet of posterboard or construction paper.

✠ *High Gothic Architecture,* http://www.bc.edu/bc_org/avp/cas/fnart/arch/chartres.html
Although there are no descriptions, the thumbnail slides (click on to enlarge) of Notre Dame Cathedral in Chartres, France, are a good visual source for cathedral features and stained glass.

69

How They Worshiped

Today you may worship at a church, a synagogue, a temple, a mosque, or not at all. In Europe during the Middle Ages, religion would have been a dominant force in your life. You would most likely have been a member of the Catholic church, but there were also Jews and Moors, who were Muslims from North Africa.

Life in the Middle Ages was difficult, and people believed that they needed the help of a higher power to make it through. The Catholics looked to God for help in this life as well as in the next. If they obeyed the rules of the church, they were promised a happy life in heaven after death. What would happen if they weren't good was spelled out in gory detail. The view of the world was absolute, with a sweet afterlife in heaven for the good and eternal torment in hell for the bad. To be good, Catholics had to go to church often, give generously to the church, confess their sins to a priest, help their neighbors, visit the sick, and give to the poor. Catholics prayed to saints who they believed would speak to God for them.

Nobles worshiped every day at the church or chapel attached to the castle. Peasants went to mass on Sunday in the parish church. There were no pews or seats. People stood for the service or brought their own stools. The mass was in Latin which few peasants spoke. Priests complained that people talked and fooled around during the service.

Churches were built of stone, and larger ones were called cathedrals. Cathedrals were huge building projects that could take one hundred years to build. There were two basic styles of cathedrals. In Romanesque architecture, big pillars and thick

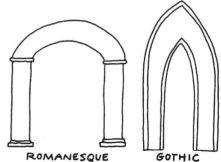

ROMANESQUE   GOTHIC

Hands-On History: Middle Ages Scholastic Professional Books

walls held up roofs with rounded arches. In the later Gothic style, the weight of the roof rested on supports outside the building called *buttresses*. The arches became sharp and pointy. Because the walls no longer had to support the weight of the roof, they were thinner and could contain large stained glass windows.

Stained Glass Windows

Stained glass windows were an important part of church decoration. They were filled with images that told stories from the Bible and illustrated the teachings of the church. Because most people couldn't read and the church services were in Latin, the stories and lessons were told through pictures.

Glass was made from a mixture of ash and washed sand. When it was heated to a very high temperature, it melted to make glass. Plain glass was a greenish color. Different metal oxides were added to make bright colors.

A stained glass window began when an artist sketched the design of the window. The next step was to make a *cartoon*, a drawing on a board or table the actual size of the window. Colored glass was then cut into shaped pieces with a hot iron tool. Sometimes pictures were drawn on the glass pieces and then fired in a kiln. Lead strips outlined the individual glass pieces and were soldered together. The window was put into an *armature*, or iron framework, and installed in an opening in the stone.

Miniature Stained Glass Window

Often miniature models of stained glass windows were made. Yours will be made by drawing on transparency film with waterproof markers. The stained glass will be set into a posterboard frame which can be shaped like a pointed arch or a rose window.

Making the Window

1. Decide whether you want to make a round rose window or an arch window. Trace the pattern on posterboard and cut out two. To cut out the center section, poke a hole in the center with the point of the scissors (ask an adult for help if you have trouble) and then cut along the inner line.

2. With a few small pieces of tape, attach the transparency film to the back of one of the frames. Make sure that the window is filled in and that the tape isn't visible from the front of the window. Trim any extra film that extends beyond the frame.

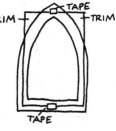

3. Decide on the design of your window. Draw your own design on a piece of paper or use one of the patterns provided.

4. Place the framed window over the design and temporarily attach it with a couple of pieces of rolled tape on the back of the frame so it doesn't slip. Trace the outlines of the design in black to look like the leading.

Hands-On History: Middle Ages Scholastic Professional Books

5. Color in the sections to look like stained glass. Be careful to keep the colors separate as they will become muddy if they mix. Fill in the background with a solid color or outline small sections to look like pieces of glass.

6. Place your window face down with the transparency film and tape on top. Put glue on the frame. Put the other frame on top and press to help it adhere. Have a paper towel on hand in case some of the glue oozes out.

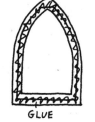

GLUE

7. If you want, you can poke a hole in the top and add a string or yarn to hang it up.

Rose Window

One of the most beautiful types of stained glass windows was the rose window. These large circular windows were so named because they resemble a rose in full bloom. Rose windows were the work of both stonemasons and stained glass craftsmen. The outline of the design was made with one of two types of stone tracery. In *plate tracery*, the design was cut into a solid sheet of stone. In *rib tracery*, the framework was created from smaller individually carved pieces. Stained glass was then set into the openings in the stone.

Your rose window uses black posterboard for the plate tracery and tissue paper for the glass.

Making the Rose Window

1. Cut a half circle from each piece of posterboard. The two halves will be pieced together when hung.

2. Plan your design on paper. Draw double lines to indicate the tracery and color them in. They should be about one inch apart. The spaces in between will contain the tissue paper, which represents the stained glass.

3. Draw your design in pencil or with white chalk on the posterboard. Put x's in the parts you will be cutting out because it can get confusing when you start cutting.

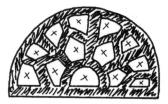

4. Cut out all the sections that will be filled in tissue paper. Poke a hole first with the end of the scissors and then cut. If you have trouble poking the holes, ask an adult for help.

5. Place the cut posterboard on the table with the side with the pencil lines facing you. Cut pieces of tissue paper in rectangles that are larger than the openings. Put the tissue paper on the opening and trace the shape about one-half inch bigger than the opening. Cut out the tissue paper. Put glue on the posterboard along the edge of the opening and attach the tissue paper.

6. Use rolled masking tape on the back to attach the stained glass to a window.

Hands-On History: Middle Ages Scholastic Professional Books

Miniature Arch Window Frame Pattern

To make a pattern, cut around outer shape, then cut out inner line.

Miniature Rose Window Patterns

Frame

To make a pattern for the miniature rose window frame, cut out around outer circle. Cut out inner circle.

Outlines

Place this under the transparency film for outlines to follow when making a miniature rose window.

Hands-On History: Middle Ages Scholastic Professional Books

Stained Glass Patterns

Resources and Readings

Reference Books

Gravett, Christopher. *Knight* (Eyewitness Books). New York: Alfred A. Knopf, 1993.
This book about knights is filled with great illustrations and lots of good information.

Hinds, Kathryn. Life in the Middle Ages series. New York: Benchmark Books, 2001.
This excellent series, filled with period illustrations, divides life in the Middle Ages into four books covering the castle, the church, the city, and the countryside. With thorough research and lots of information, it is best suited to the higher grades. Bits of poetry and Chaucer are sprinkled throughout.

Langley, Andrew. *Medieval Life* (Eyewitness Books). New York: Alfred A. Knopf, 1996.
Presenting the visual flavor of life at the time, this is a good classroom resource.

MacDonald, Fiona. *How Would You Survive in the Middle Ages?* New York: Franklin Watts, 1995.
This accessible book with lots of information has nicely laid-out pages on a variety of topics including home, family, food, clothes, sports and games, and government. The information is simple enough for younger students but has enough details for older students.

Steele, Philip. *Castles*. New York: Kingfisher, 1995.
This simply written, well illustrated book offers a guide to life in the castle in the Middle Ages.

Wilson, Elizabeth B. *Bibles and Bestiaries: A Guide to Illuminated Manuscripts for Young Readers*. New York: Farrar, Straus and Giroux, 1994.
This clearly written book is beautifully illustrated with examples from manuscripts in the Pierpont Morgan Library in New York. It includes a detailed description of the creation of an illuminated manuscript from making the vellum to binding the books.

Picture Books

Aliki. *A Medieval Feast*. New York: Harper & Row, 1983.
Aliki's charmingly illustrated book tells the story of Camdenton Manor as it prepares and serves a feast for the visiting king.

Clements, Gillian. *The Truth About Castles*. Minneapolis, MN: Carolrhoda Books, Inc., 1990.
Lots of information about castles and medieval life is conveyed with a sense of humor in this visual book with a comic book feel.

Hodges, Margaret. *Saint George and the Dragon*, illustrated by Trina Schart Hyman. Boston: Little, Brown, and Company, 1984.
This retelling of the story of Saint George and the dragon from Edmund Spenser's *Faerie Queene* has exquisite illustrations with wonderful borders by Trina Schart Hyman.

Hunt, Jonathan. *Illuminations*. New York: Aladdin Books, 1993.
Illuminated letters of the alphabet give information about the Middle Ages from alchemist to zither. This book is filled with interesting tidbits of information and beautiful illustrations.

Macaulay, David. *Cathedral: The Story of Its Construction*. Boston: Houghton Mifflin Company, 1973.
Macaulay, David. *Castle*. Boston: Houghton Mifflin Company, 1977.
Detailed information on the building of a cathedral and a castle is presented in an engaging way with distinctive pen and ink illustrations. There are also videos available.

O'Brien, Patrick. *The Making of a Knight: How Sir James Earned His Armor*. Watertown, MA: Charlesbridge Publishing, 1998.
Seven-year-old James leaves his parents' home to become a page. Fourteen years later he becomes a knight. Lots of facts about the process are woven into the story.

Platt, Richard. *Castle Diary: The Journal of Tobias Burgess, Page*, illustrated by Chris Riddell. Cambridge, MA: Candlewick Press, 1999.
This large format picture book is the diary of Tobias Burgess's first year as a page in 1285. Lots of information about daily life and special occasions in the castle is presented in an entertaining way.

Robertson, Bruce. *Marguerite Makes a Book*, illustrated by Kathryn Hewitt. Los Angeles, J. Paul Getty Museum, 1999.
This beautifully illustrated picture book tells of Marguerite, a girl in medieval Paris. Her father illuminates books and she helps him finish an important commission of a Book of Hours for Lady Isabelle.

Fiction

Cushman, Karen. *Catherine Called Birdy*. New York: HarperTrophy, 1994.
Feisty Catherine begins her diary in September 1290. Her strong personality and irreverent view of life around her makes for pleasant company and a feeling for life in the Middle Ages. Please note that her earthy comments may not be for everyone.

de Angeli, Marguerite. *The Door in the Wall*. Garden City, New York: Doubleday & Company, 1949.
Full of period detail, this heartwarming story is about Robin, a ten-year-old boy whose hopes of becoming a knight are crushed when an illness makes him lame. He overcomes his handicap and spoiled nature to become a hero.

Gray, Elizabeth Janet. *Adam of the Road*. New York: The Viking Press, 1942.
Adam, the eleven-year-old son of the minstrel Roger, is separated from his father and his beloved dog, Nick, and has many adventures as he searches for them both. This is a great story with glimpses of life in a monastery school, a castle, a city, a farm, and a university.

Temple, Frances. *The Ramsay Scallop*. New York: Orchard Books, 1994.
Fourteen-year-old Elenor, and Thomas, her betrothed who has returned from the Crusades, are sent by the village priest on a pilgrimage from England to Spain to atone for the sins of the village. While they have many adventures along the way, the romantic elements of the story make it most appropriate for older girls.

For Teachers

Books

Cosman, Madeleine Pesner. *Fabulous Feasts: Medieval Cookery and Ceremony*. New York: George Braziller, 1976.
This book contains detailed information on medieval cooking and serving, as well as suggestions for presenting a feast and recipes.

Gies, Frances and Joseph. *Life in a Medieval Village*. New York: Harper & Row, 1990.
Gies, Frances and Joseph. *Life in a Medieval Castle*. New York: Harper & Row, 1974.
Gies, Frances and Joseph. *Life in a Medieval City*. New York: Harper & Row, 1969.
These are well-written and thorough texts on aspects of medieval life. Some sections bog down with lists and details but most of it is an enjoyable read.

Web Sites

Dover Books
http://www.doverpublications.com
Their coloring books, stencils, iron-on transfers, and clip art are useful visual resources.

The Internet Connection for Medieval Resources
http://www.netserf.org
This Web site has well organized and clearly displayed links to Medieval resources on the Internet.

Society for Creative Anachronism
http://www.sca.org
Here are lots of links and information about the Society for Creative Anachronism, which is comprised of people interested in medieval recreation and reenactment.